My Only Crime

ALSO FROM *POETS & TRAITORS* PRESS

Advances in Embroidery by Ahmad Al-Ashqar
Relative Genitive by Val Vinokur
Education by Windows by Johnny Lorenz
A Life Replaced by Olga Livshin
Other Shepherds by Nina Kossman
Ambivalent Souls by Robert E. Tanner
Means To Be Lucky by Annie Kantar

My Only Crime

*Poems, Translations, Lives,
and Akhmatova's Requiem*

Richard Lourie

Copyright © 2024 by Richard Lourie.
All rights reserved.

Published 2024 in New York by Poets & Traitors Press
www.poets-traitors.com
poetstraitors@gmail.com

Editors: Val Vinokur, Katya Danziger

Published in the United States of America.

Poets & Traitors Press is an independent publisher of books of poetry and translations by a single author/translator. The press emerged from the Poet/Translator Reading Series and from the New School's Literary Translation Workshop to showcase authors who travel between writing and translation, artists for whom Language is made manifest through languages and whose own word carries, shapes, and is shaped by that of another.

Poets & Traitors Press acknowledges support from Eugene Lang College, the New School Bachelor's Program for Adults and Transfer Students, and the New School Foreign Languages Department.

ISBN: 978-0-9990737-7-3

To Jod who stayed and to Jim who left

My Only Crime

CONTENTS

Grandfathered In — 17

I.

Pre-Natal Self Portrait — 26
Admission — 27
My Father as a Foreigner — 28
Namesake — 29
Adam *by Evgeny Vinokurov* — 30
Legacy *by Henryk Grynberg* — 31
First Love — 32
Joyriding '54 — 33
Eighteen Years Old *by Naum Korzhavin* — 34
A Word — 35
The Too-Young Married Girl — 36
Scuba 1 — 37
Icarus — 38
Last Swim at Walden — 39
Preview — 40
Oct — 41
The Sentry — 42

II.

What Have You Taught Me, Robert Lowell? — 46
Home For a Visit — 47
Emily Dickinson Considers the Speed of Light — 48
Dylan Thomas Filching Dress Shirts from His Host — 49
Boston Without You — 50

Untitled *by Alexander Pushkin*   52
Question of the Day   54
At The Hopper Retrospective   55
Painting versus Poetry   56
A Grammatical Quickie   57
Sketch of a Friend   58
Postcard from the Vineyard   59
4th.   60
A Carpenter   61
Dawn Through Three Windows   62
Japanese Archery *by Aleksander Wat*   63
To Robinson Jeffers *by Czeslaw Milosz*   64
Reading Rexroth's Translation of Tu Fu   66
The Ghost of Delmore Schwartz   67
Worms   68
A Day Without Poetry   70

III.

Victory Day   72
The Linguist Declining a Romance at an International
      Conference   73
Fear of Heights   74
Stains   75
To The Translator *by Vyacheslav Ivanov*   76
Five Sonnets from "Eugene Onegin"
      by Alexander Pushkin   77
Eulogy for Dale Landers   82
The Gambler   83

Perestroika	84
To Janis Joplin	85
The Con Artist	86
The Sixth Sense *by Nikolai Gumilev*	87
Stoppage	88
Tolstoy at Fifty	89
The Poisoner	90
You Who Wronged *by Czeslaw Milosz*	91
Ode On the Death of Yuri Andropov	92
A Fable	93

IV.

Requiem *by Anna Akhmatova*	96

V.

In The Bookstore	114
The Greek Restaurant	115
Metaphysical	116
The Self-Pitier	117
Temptation of the Rabbi	118
The Ghost Speaks	119
End of the Marriage	120
Hymn To Nothing	121
Vision	122
Psychic Again	123
The Widows of Boca Raton	124
Fishian	126
Dracula's Apology	128

Lives of the Poets

Evgeny Vinokurov	130
Henryk Grynberg	131
Naum Korzhavin	132
Alexander Pushkin	133
Aleksander Wat	135
Czeslaw Milosz	137
Vyacheslav Ivanov	139
Nikolai Gumilev	140
Anna Akhmatova	141

PREVIOUSLY PUBLISHED

"Tolstoy at Fifty" in ORUS, 1995

"The Self-Pitier" in The New Criterion, October 1994

"What Have You Taught Me, Robert Lowell?" in The New Criterion, June 1991.

"The Ghost of Delmore Schwartz" in Ploughshares, Spring 1981.

"A Day Without Poetry" in Ploughshares, Fall 1977

"Stains" in Hyperion, December 1974

"Temptation of the Rabbi" in Response, Spring 1973

"Worms" in Amphora No. 7, 1972

"The Too-Young Married Girl" in Reflections, Spring 1965

GRANDFATHERED IN

I was slightly drunk and asleep when I was arrested. The tall Soviet policeman touched my shoulder to wake me and said in a scarily polite voice: "Would you be so kind as to come with me?"

I was in a train station in Gori, the hometown of Joseph Stalin in Georgia.

And I was about to find out why my father always gave a one-word answer to my questions about what it was like in Russia when he was a boy, and that one word was: "Terrible."

If he had told me a few stories I might have been satisfied and stopped asking, but, as it was, I was frustrated, intrigued.

His father, Natan, a blacksmith, chose to move to America where his grandchildren would laugh at him for wearing his hat inside the house.

Did he think Russia was terrible too? Terrible how? And how terrible?

I'd never know because he never spoke English.

My other grandfather, Peter, had come from Russia with just his cobbler's tools, which he always kept with him. One night while courting my grandmother on the subway – a bag of roast chestnuts and a ride, all the outing they could afford — they were threatened near the end of the line by a pistol-wielding anti-Semite. The tools my grandfather always had with him now proved useful in other than their usual ways. He cut the man's face open from scalp to chin with his linoleum knife. Sixty years later my grandmother still wept hearing the story retold.

Peter got rich quick in get-rich-quick America, owning a good-sized shoe factory on the north shore of Massachusetts. He smoked Cuban cigars and drove glossy black Cadillacs

When I asked him about Russia, he was only too happy to regale me with tales of horse-traders and horse thieves, gypsies and pails of vodka, of Russians who wore their pants tucked inside their boots and slept on stoves. One night, fetching wood, the door locked behind him and he watched a pack of wolves march through the chest-deep snow. He stood there afraid to breathe 'til they were gone.

He taught me my first Russian, only two phrases but enough to catch some part of a boy's deep attention and start some unseen process that would only surface later. Those phrases were – "Dai mnie papirosoo" and "Potseluy menya na zhopoo" meaning. "Give me a cigarette" and "Kiss my ass."

I was off and running.

Announcing at seventeen that I was a poet and could not therefore attend pharmacy college and inherit my father's two drugstores, I somehow got into Boston University where two life-changing events would occur. I read Crime and Punishment, which gave me both nightmares and moments of exaltation. If it was so powerful in translation, what must the original be like? I signed up for Beginner's Russian.

Also, Robert Lowell was at that time offering a poetry-writing class, but only for upperclassmen and graduate students. I, of course, was neither. But there was one other way into his class – by his direct approval. That meant going to see him, poems in hand, and wait with my head bowed for the axe of rejection.

Lowell greeted me quite graciously and even offered me half of his tuna fish sandwich, but how could I, a mere supplicant, a non-entity of youth, accept a portion of a god's food? Then Lowell's attention was focused entirely on the sheets of typescript I had handed him.

"The first line alone will get you in," said Lowell, then quoted me to me: "The black wood of October trees…"

Lowell was sane that year and a good teacher. He'd pass out poems printed in purple mimeograph ink with no other information – we had to figure out, just from the reading of the poem itself, whether it was an original or a translation and explain how we reached our conclusion. Was it contemporary and, if not, when was it written? Was the author a man or a woman? This was pure reading without any of the hints of context and culture.

Midway through the semester Lowell announced he would be judging a poetry contest and presenting to the winner the Sneath Poetry Award, which also came with a handsome twenty-five-dollar prize. It was open to the Boston University community, us, of course, included.

The last class came on a humid June day and as we gathered up our books and papers one last time, Lowell had still made no announcement. Maybe it had been called off, or postponed for lack of anything talented enough.

Walking down a cement stairwell beside me, Lowell suddenly stopped and pulled a crinkled envelope from his inside jacket pocket which he handed to me, saying: "I almost forgot. You won."

No honor has eclipsed it since.

Lowell also suggested that I come by his office for a little chat about my future now that I appeared to have one.

In that last chat Lowell told me what lay ahead for me as an up-and-coming poet. "You'll major in English literature," he said, "you'll publish in the little magazines, you'll go on to grad school and write a thesis on Dryden or The Fairie Queen or something of the sort, then go on to teach creative writing and English composition…"

Outwardly self-possessed and in awe of him as ever, inwardly I was shouting, "Oh no, oh no, oh no I won't, I'll go to California and study Russian, and read Dostoevsky and live by my pen!"

By a suspicious coincidence, I arrived in Berkeley just as the emigre Polish poet Czeslaw Milosz joined the faculty of UC's Slavic Department, to which I had transferred. He and my father had been born only miles apart in the Lithuanian part of the Tsarist empire.

A few days after a reading of poetry by faculty and students of the Slavic department, myself included, reading "The Prodigal Son"– "Weeping and weeping / He falls to his knees / And has not repented…"– Milosz took me aside and said in his magnificent Slavic brogue, "It has been decided to help you, Lurye", pronouncing my name old-country style. "We know you are married and have a child, and so starting tomorrow you are officially in charge of the mimeograph machine."

When I reported to work the next day the two Russian women secretaries told me in no uncertain terms– "There is only one rule about the mimeograph, no poet is ever going to lay a hand on it."

"So, what should I do then?"

"Sit down and have a cup of tea."

I would drink hundreds of cups of tea and talk endless hours with the secretaries who called me Richard Samoilovich (my patronymic). I learned more Russian there than in any classroom where emigres explicated gerunds.

His dark blue raincoat over his shoulders like a cape, Milosz cut a dashing figure on campus. He was known in European and American circles as the author of The Captive Mind, a penetrating analysis of the inner contortions of the Eastern European intelligentsia as they attempted to adjust to the new reality of communism. But his poetry was practically unknown outside of those who had read it in the original.

We started translating poetry (his and others') in his study that smelled of burnt tobacco and old books. It was a master-apprentice relationship. He would insist that a more perfect version existed, if only we would not be satisfied with the merely "quite good" and strive toward the excellent. He once astonished me by saying, "This line is a little too smooth, we need to roughen it up a bit." I had no idea that lines could be too smooth, let alone that it was possible to roughen them up.

At one point Milosz mentioned quite casually, "You know, Richard, you could make a living by translating."

He was right. It wasn't much of a living, but in America in the seventies and eighties, the exigencies of the Cold War meant that there was always money sloshing around for translation projects on the Know-Thy-Enemy principle. And translation work bought me time to write.

From the start I could see that translating from Russian was going to involve more than just turning the words of one language into those of another. This was clear when I began translating Andrei Sakharov's Memoirs, which he was writing from internal exile in the closed city of Gorky. The KGB had already stolen the nearly thousand-page manuscript from him twice, and twice he had simply begun again from the beginning. And so, each time I was handed a new segment by Sakharov's son-in-law and fellow dissident Efrem Yankelevich, he would say: "Top Secret. Burn Before Reading."

I smuggled in, I smuggled out. Without quite meaning to, I had discovered a huge hole in Moscow airport customs for departing passengers – your luggage was X-rayed and OKed before you went to the check-in counter where the bag would be put on the conveyor belt. If you could manage to transfer something from your person to the bag in the milling chaos in front of the counter, it would be on its way stateside.

I became adept at smuggling white-out. The dissidents typed all their underground publications with multiple sheets of carbon paper and needed the white-out to correct typos. I once happened to deliver a case of white-out in a blizzard and for a time among a small circle of refuseniks, it became proverbial: to deliver white-out in a blizzard.

Knowing I would one day want to write about Stalin, I travelled illegally to his hometown of Gori in the mountains of Georgia in March 1988. I did not have the right to go outside the Georgian capital Tbilisi and had to leave my passport at my hotel. But I wanted to see what Stalin saw as a child stepping out from his home, a two-room brick hovel that did not even have an inside connecting door but had now been encased in grandiose marble. After a long and somewhat nervous day, I drank a good bottle of Georgian white wine with a tasty dinner before dozing off in the waiting room for the last train back to the capital. And it was then that the tall Soviet policeman asked me if I would be so kind as to go with him.

He took me to a long, narrow, bare-walled room where I was interrogated by six men whose leader kept repeating: "You have no identification, you're travelling with a high-speed camera, you speak perfect Russian, what do YOU think WE think YOU are?"

My Russian was in some ways better than theirs, and at times I was worried that they may not have mastered the subjunctive sufficiently to realize that "I would have done" does not mean "I did". But that only made the challenge all the greater. I was not only arguing for my freedom, but perhaps my very life. Another phrase the leader repeated with feigned concern was – "And what if, God forbid, something happened to you, we wouldn't know where to send your body."

One thing I understood at once, instinctively, was that these men were masters at detecting lies, half lies, prevarications, and bullshit of any sort. They could hear it in the very timbre of a voice. And so, from the very start I made no secret of what was in fact my true aim in being there – to write about their great local hero, Joseph Stalin. That perked them all up. They wanted to know "what the West in general and I in particular" thought about the great Generalissimo Stalin. They were gladdened to hear of our respect for his industrialization of the country but grew a little hostile and suspicious if I seemed to be overdoing the praise and so then

I would switch to a critique of his methods, the tragedy of collectivization and forced labor, but they didn't want to hear much of that for long, and so I'd move on to Stalin's victorious role in WWII until their eyes began to narrow again. Then the five underlings would bark questions and insults at me, until their boss reined them back in.

At the worst moments I feared that I had foolishly translated myself back to that reality my forefathers were so anxious to flee and would soon find out exactly what my father meant by "terrible."

But at the best moments there was a keen existential thrill, a madcap euphoria, for what could be better than dueling for your very life and doing it in the Russian language and in Stalin's hometown? And not only that but winning! In the end they saw me off, wishing me a safe and pleasant journey.

If I had followed in my father's footsteps and become a pharmacist, or even an assistant professor of creative writing as Lowell predicted, then the life I've actually lived would have just been a path untaken and I would never have been interrogated in that train station in what was, and remains, the best evening of my life.

— Richard Lourie
Venice, California and San Miguel de Allende, Mexico

I.

PRE-NATAL SELF-PORTRAIT

A near zero you doze in utero.
Your sex, your scent, the color of your eyes
are still unknown but all the same
in the sky and living room
your zodiac takes form around you,
slowing like a roulette wheel
seeking the click of specific selection.

Standing dreamy by the window,
one hand on the bulge of you,
watching a sun-lit cloud pass
over red brick and green trees,
your mother suddenly turns to see
Isabelle beside her, a finger pressed to her lips.

Isabelle must rush her blessing
in the urgent whisper
sisters use to share their secrets:
may women love your son,
may his luck hold till the end,
and may he be one of those
who, unreminded, remember us, the dead.

ADMISSION

I belong to the Jews.
They came for me at birth.
With a scalpel of prayer
they cut my flesh around.

They took me home.
A mother and a father poured
their voices through my ears
until, my own voice naming, I awoke.

I was taken to their hidden year
where bare time is decorated
into a journey of common memory
by sweet wine, old books, and bitter herbs.

I fled from them into Egypt.
And in Egypt took a bride.
No one knew my name in Egypt.
In Egypt no one claimed my flesh.

Jews stand in my sleep reciting dreams,
melting like candles into darkness
when morning light touches my forehead
gently as an ancient hand.

I belong to the Jews.
They will take me at the end.

MY FATHER AS A FOREIGNER

Faces streaked a fog of overcoats
that murmured a babel of stinks.
My father crossed Lethe in steerage —
gulping air that tasted like grief.

Jokes, proverbs, songs, scoured to oblivion,
sea-sickness became their common tongue.
The apple tree, the well, the village square –
fata morganas against drizzle and swell.

The bare odor of abandonment
called rats and spiders to his house.
On tiptoe children peered in through windows
at the emptiness cornered by walls.

The living vanish better than the dead,
they leave no graves or furniture behind.
The shades stampeded to the gangplank,
then filed into the promised land.

But that little town still designed his hunger,
calling for sour cream, onions, black bread.
And he sipped his tea through lump sugar
that ate his teeth like time made sweet.

Perhaps his dying was so arduous and long
because his youth was rooted an ocean away
in Raguva where the hard-won fields went straight
from the woods down to the Jew-hating streets.

NAMESAKE

Born in the reign of the next to last tsar,
My grandfather loved snow, vodka and wolves,
But his own father peered across oceans.
Said the writing on the wall: DEATH TO JEWS.

My grandfather got rich in get-rich America
And did it quick which made it twice as good.
He drove black Cadillacs and married up.
"Three" was always "tree" on his migrant lips.

Daughter after daughter but not a son
Until one was born so far before his time
He was just three minutes in vivacious air,
Not worth all the nuisance of a name.

Never to be born is the greatest luck,
Said the Greeks, next best is death just after birth.
Lucky you who were never you,
And who, nameless, ended the Kantor name.

Learning of you a century later,
Touched and aggrieved by your fate,
I, by the powers vested in me
By poetry's unacknowledged legislature,

Do hereby name you Richard,
My own name and so mine to give,
Unlucky me who dallied for decades
In this world of rockets and acacias.

ADAM

By Evgeny Vinokurov

Having looked all around with an easy gaze,
matting the grass as he walked that first day,
he lay down in the shade of a fig tree
and fell asleep, his hands behind his head.
His sleep was sweet and deep and trouble free
beneath the blue peace of Eden's sky.
....In his dream he saw the ovens at Auschwitz
and ditches piled high with the dead.
It was his own children he saw! But in the bliss
of paradise his face shone brightly with a smile.
And he slept on, understanding nothing of this,
not knowing as yet of good and evil.

Translated from the Russian

LEGACY

By Henryk Grynberg

You did not leave me your kingdom
You did not leave me your temple
You did not leave believers
You did not even leave me your faith
You did not even leave me the dead
unless you count the fading call of the void
in the cleft air above my head

You did not leave me retaliation
I don't even know who to shoot at
from my poor sling
or what the murderer's name is –
Million
or Ten Million
You left me no friends after all
So why leave me enemies

And why did you so lavishly
make me the heir
to every quiver
of every last worn string
of your harp
of isolation
and vile unkingly suffering
O David...

Warsaw, 1967
Translated from the Polish

FIRST LOVE

Cautiously, like humankind,
stepping into the future
a day at a time,
I,
at the age of eleven, entered
a sea mist of Irish slums,
alert for gangs of angry brothers,
their heads shaved for ringworm,
their fists hard as radiators,
some Catholic fish hook in their guts,
And I crossed line after line to kiss Margaret
in my first treason to boys and Jews.

That I should see you once again
in the half-life after childhood
so startled me, Margaret,
it took me these twenty years to say "Hello".

JOYRIDING '54

For Gerry Bergstein

When the air is still as pavement,
then it's time to break and enter.

High on no drug but the crime,
this isn't done for pals or girls,
or to flash later like a blue tattoo
emblazoned on a deltoid.

In the act before the action,
he finds the will to shatter voices –
of his mother and the priests.
After that, the door's a snap.

His Wop do D.A.ed, a J. D.
in dungarees and a clean white T-
shirt, his fingers boogie hotwiring the V-
8, sure beats a night of beer and T.V.

Leaving the skunk stink of rubber
down onramps, he laughs from 0 to 60,
the trees and evening one darkness now
except for apparitions thumbing rides.

Caring neither for profit nor destruction,
the two great hobbies of the world,
he streaks past rest-stops and speed-traps,
in elations of larceny and internal combustion.

And even the sirens behind him
seem to be keening his freedom.

EIGHTEEN YEARS OLD

By Naum Korzhavin

Every word from my mouth is evidence
That could cost me ten years at the least.
Through a Moscow rife with spies and informers
I walk with the true poet's strut.

No need for all that tailing and surveilling!
And a shame to waste scarce paper on my file!
And, as for compromising material,
My very existence is itself nothing but.

1944
Translated from the Russian

A WORD

Without a word the women know –
Not this one, not that one,
he does not love us as we are,
his heart is bent against us in some way.

But this one, this one is at his ease
with little girls and grandmamas,
what we all were and all with luck become.
He does not only wish to drink you down

and for a week be drunk on you.
This one will sip you day by day,
and let himself in turn be sipped.
He's worth the danger of a word.

THE TOO-YOUNG MARRIED GIRL

The peasant goes across the muddy yard
To hang her laundry on the fence.

—*Alexander Pushkin*

Where her jaws are hinged there is the taste
green apples give. The bottom has fallen out
of her attention to her lap, her hands
pursue a floral chain in needlepoint's fine tedium.
Hogs rummage for leftovers in the mud
beneath her window, the fence, the field
and its disassociated noise ripple softly
like the too hot summer air. In repetition
and agenda there is comfort, life goes on.
One year of marriage not yet complete and already
she is to bear fruit in autumn like any tree.
The cry of infants through bleak sleep,
the husband's grunt, the candle glare
on the small and ugly face, illusions
are too dear, the cow's mild days
and the fate of chickens are to be envied.
She has lately dreamt of wells and spiders and awoken
upright beside her husband taut with her skin
and feared no fatal blushing illness
would be her knight against old age.
As if possessed, the ceaseless needle pricks
a single drop of blood out from a finger
and the slightest cry of pain becomes her voice.

SCUBA 1

for Rob/Gav

Disguised as a seal by science,
rubber flesh scarred by neoprene,
I slip into the pressure
which triples every hundred feet,
a strict and lethal rule.

Now, free of allegiance to the vertical,
nearly happy but for the gauges,
I hunt where no saints have gazed
except for the statues in shipwrecks.

If the tank on my back is a lung,
then what is this gun in my hand?
A hypodermic for civilized poisons,
a retired caveman's totem,
a twisted secret no straighter in steel?

Those are land questions. Here,
where everything is sidelong and saline,
life eats life alive
and I worship God as Zero Mercy.

ICARUS

to Gavril

We have not been told the whole story of Icarus.
Tradition leaves him drowning in the dazzling sea,
but in fact he was saved by a fisherman
so used to seeing goddesses
stepping from moonlight to cross a grove
or laughing iridescently in the spray
the wind lifts from breaking waves,
he did not think it strange at all
that a boy should plunge from the sky
to break melting wings and arms
on a Wednesday afternoon.

Healed by secret herbs and weeks of sleep,
Icarus pecked at the shell of coma
until he awoke to white-washed walls
and arched windows blue with ocean day.

In time he took a liking to the island folk
and, no longer tempted by flight
and wise to the might of the sun,
he stayed on with them, embraced their ways,
and married one man's daughter, as all men do.

When his own son was of a certain age
and Icarus could see
the disposition of his youth reborn in him,
he had to struggle long
and hard to say the words:
Yes, I know, my son, go try your wings.

LAST SWIM AT WALDEN

to Jod

The smell of warm light on dirt
is exactly the same as when we were children,
the path of dry shadow still covered
with pine needles, golden, iodine-red.

Roots trips us. Bearing food
and the serious toys of our leisure,
we descend to the sky-colored water.
Not believing in change, we have changed.

Like a sister who never found happiness,
the pond receives us, guests
neither welcome nor unwelcome.
For a hour, an hour or two,
we sidestroke and cavort like dolphins,
our wiser cousins,
who abandoned the land and hard labor
for witty repartee and arcades of play,
philosophe dolphins,
all forehead and grin like Voltaire.

Alternating speech and silence,
we roll our towels, cap the thermos,
as a wind from Canada or October
sends waves of goose-flesh across the pond.
Now, on the way back up the hill,
I judge the broken twigs as kindling.

PREVIEW

October's binocular clarity
focuses the red edge of brick
into the present tense of air and eye,
and renders each blue degree
of the punt's arc
which pauses to savor its zenith.

Soon it will come,
what northerners love –
the long cave of evening,
a kitchen lit by lamps and kinship,
darkness with the weight of snow.

OCT

One good rain takes all of autumn's beauty, one cold
long night and morning of insistent rain
and all October's affluence of scarlet and gold
is down on lawns, in gutters, down the drain.

Fallen stocks in the market of the year,
currency worthless after war, yellow, wet scarlet,
the leaves like glossies strewn about by a starlet
rushed to the hospital after an aborted career.

The sky's exact grey is so painfully slight
that it would be hard to breathe were it air
and stands as still as the passionless despair
of a spirit failing in its own woken sight.

But June will rise from these dead leaves and black sticks.
New England's not deceived. We know these tricks.

THE SENTRY

for Judy Haberl

I sleep. He does not sleep.
I dream of the dead smiling
in stores they used to own.
He listens to the color
of the night for the assailant,
for danger's code – the cry of glass,
lament of ambulance. I sleep.
I dream of money found.

Even in that landscape
of my true joy and terror
which the blind soul cannot see
except in pictures of the world,
another sentry goes with me
and when a thief digs
his knife into my helpless wrist,
that sentry whispers in my ear
the only verb he knows –
the imperative of to wake.

Reincarnated by newsprint and egg yolks,
I leave home's stairs and gas stoves safe,
shadowed by a perfect agent
down the long streets of the day.
Physicist of every menace,
he plots distance and velocity --
the sleepy citizen, the speed-demon cab --
and when his bat-cry of sonar
rebounds off a showroom it sounds
like a friend shouting my name.

Invisible in every mirror but this,
exposable on no other film,
my spectral sentries even now
stand behind my shoulder
like parents watching through a window
as their child runs across the grass
missing nearly every single rusty nail.

II.

WHAT HAVE YOU TAUGHT ME, ROBERT LOWELL?

Between the ball scores and the weather
(Boston slips a game behind, cloudy with a chance of rain)
they give your death one well-enunciated line,
Memento Mori on Channel Five.

And it did rain on the first day
of the world without you, the first day
of the New Year of the Jews, my Jews,
of whom I was the first son to speak
that language which was always yours,
though none of us could ever own
that Harvardian Back Bay Virginia drawl,
even those among us seeking final hygiene
in Pilgrim wives and studies of The Faerie Queen.

The Russian Jews, the steerage Jews, the Chelsea Jews,
blending piety and greed to produce ambition
and the longing to speak perfect English
on which I apparently O.D.'ed.
When I informed my father I would forsake
pharmacy for poetry, we both knew
something broke. The language came between us.
We argued on for years but never really spoke.

HOME FOR A VISIT

After the garrulous epiphanies of grandsons
whose smiles and eyes are likened to unlikely cousins
and others lost in bags of photos or moved away,
after dinner and the dishes, the husbands retire
to the flagstone porch to speak of matters
which, save death, are purely local.

The square screen walls of the porch
peninsula the backyard dark where sprinklers coldly lash
and starlight falls into a baseball glove,
a perfect catch. The highway drone thins.
Assorted lepidoptera dart in the bulb light.
The last awake, I scavenge what outlives the day.

EMILY DICKINSON CONSIDERS THE SPEED OF LIGHT

The sun I see up in the sky
was really there a while ago,
and if its fires had gone awry,
I'd be among the last to know.

In the mirror— the Self I perceive
is younger than my living eye.
Were I quite suddenly to die,
would She have time enough to grieve?

Light excels at graceful haste —
Seven times round the planet's waist
in one second's time. Ricocheting off the moon,
it pauses here in Amherst at high noon

And makes the lawns glow a deeper green
and lights the page so I can read.
All that must be what people mean
when wishing you Godspeed.

DYLAN THOMAS FILCHING DRESS SHIRTS FROM HIS HOST

Downstairs, procreation's unceasing buzz of lies.
Up in the bedroom, Thomas, lip-protrudingly,
weighs the pale blue against the solid green:

"Blue's good for dignity or occasions,
and for a certain quietude as well,
a shirt, after a few washes, you could write in.

"But the green's strictly for carousing,
a glass in one hand, an ass in the other,
your lips only able to kiss and speak truth.

"And what are we if not the progeny of thieves —
Adam, Prometheus, Genghis Khan,
stealing apples, Fire, continents galore.

"And poetry's not a whit less larcenous,
shoplifting time from life's agendaed day
to make the stanzas it sells for a song.

"But who needs justification, better just to say –
On my way to piss I stumbled on a treasure trove
and, Sweet Jesus, the sleeves not even half a size short!"

BOSTON WITHOUT YOU

for Diane Wolf

Your death has made the river bluer
and bared the nerve that hears the wind
move among deciduous June leaves
as new generations graduate and marry.

Watercolor Boston, blue and green,
along one long uneven stroke of red,
city of lawyers and surgeons
who can only sometimes save us

from our crimes and those committed
by the same great force,
lovely and sinister beyond human reason,
that makes the earth lift and open

to the day like a secretary
sunning herself by the river, the pages
of her book catching the noon light
to flash blank in perfect amnesia.

Oblong mattresses emerge from dorms.
Gypsy moths descend on glinting strings.
In that year, that was to be the last,
I think you knew the freedom and the love
that so few of us in fact prefer.
And then you went ahead of everyone,
stranding us like fathers in a waiting room.

I am no different from this city
or this season, forgetful, so in love
with blue and green, but today your ghost
is close to me, unearthly white,
a bride dashing to a limousine.

UNTITLED

By Alexander Pushkin

Whether I wander the clamorous streets
Or step inside a thronged cathedral
Or sit among the mad-cap young,
I give myself to reverie,

And tell myself the years will race
And all of us seen here today
Shall face the same eternal arch –
And someone's hour is close at hand.

Gazing at a solitary oak
I know this forest patriarch
Will outlive my soon forgotten time
As it outlived our fathers' day and age.

And when I hold an infant in my arms,
I cannot help but think, Farewell,
I yield my place to you.
Your time to flower is mine to fade.

And it is now the habit of my mind
To look upon each passing day
And try to guess what date will be
The anniversary to my coming death.

And where will fate send me that death?
In battle, travel or at sea?
Or will a valley close to home
Receive my cold remains?

Though flesh that can no longer feel
Can hardly care where it decays,
I still prefer to rest
Near places dearest to my heart.

And by the entrance to my tomb
May youthful life forever play
And nature's deathless beauty shine,
In ray after indifferent ray.

December 26, 1829
Translated from the Russian

QUESTION OF THE DAY

And if this were to be the day,
not as I had hoped —
at home, serene, free of pain,
belled in an amplitude of farewell,

but here in midtown amid
the honking of impacted hastes,
dayglo graffiti of pedestrians seen
through cab windows dim with grime,
the cost of time and motion rising
in red numbers made of light
that flickers like the pulse at a broker's cuff,
a cursing stranger at the wheel,

could I, in the mind's last tide, say —
It was achieved, I die rich.

April 13, 1994

AT THE HOPPER RETROSPECTIVE

Familiar from New England lakes,
that sudden cold, colder for its suddenness,
four feet before each picture where
the man had stepped back from his easel.

In one painting, of a theater, the curtain,
heavy with velvet and reluctance, will soon rise
upon a family's life, a kitchen
busy with unhappiness. In another,
a solitary reader on a train
is about to raise her eyes
to the long movie of the night and see
behind her face reflected in the window
a stranger enter, pausing not to startle.
In a third, beside an unlit house, the road
bears nothing on to the distant sky.

Facts in daylight's nihilistic brilliance,
exact solitudes in suits, they have
a stark ease and yet are tense
with the verge precise outline implies.

Surely, any moment now, the stranger
in her compartment will turn and tell
her of her worth and value,
his every sentence shattering her silence
like firemen axing the windshield as you bleed.

April 7, 1994

PAINTING VERSUS POETRY

On the walls of mansions and museums
The originals vividly unique,
Almost what the painter himself beheld
Say four centuries from Friday last,
Except for the ripple of fresh judgement glinting in pigment
And the light of place that swells and holds
Just before the present becomes the past.

Unlike ubiquity, uniqueness requires expedition,
Art is to be lugged like luggage,
Curated, crated, and insured
Against heists, tsunamis, flame and civil war
And the wear and tear of admiration's gaze.
But it is readers who get the last laugh –
An original Shakespeare for a buck and a half!

A GRAMMATICAL QUICKIE

I met her in an improper noun
frequented by those who live
in that old, tight-hearted town,
and, oh, her lips were adjective.

Somehow I found the words to say
that the future of "to be"
was best conjugated by her and me,
and so we verbed the night away.

Since no present can ever last,
all that is now in the perfect past,
though memories of her, laughing, nude,
still shift me to subjunctive mood.

SKETCH OF A FRIEND

To him
life was a sweet sadness,
a Jewish wine.

Remember
the charred ruins of the crime
as the waitress sets down the red glass,
Remember
the ashes of tragedy,
an asterisk of light on her ring.

Half-life of ash and cinder
shimmer in this June,
drift and fall into his wine
which he then half raises in a toast:

To love this life
fully and completely,
is a sin against memory,
this life
a night
in which the innocents
are pursued and slaughtered,
night followed by a market day,
voices calling prices,
hands grabbing fruit,
flies drunk on meat smoke,
voices still calling prices
as night falls, darkness
riding the sound of hooves.

POSTCARD FROM THE VINEYARD

The winter coats are hung in the closet
where time and umbrellas stand still.
The world turns the mainland away. The waves,
creatures rough, simple and dumb, bear us
to isolation, pagan August, and porches
painted the same white as shells and gulls.

Where all religions fail, the beach succeeds.
Men surrender rank, and the cells sick
with nicotine and anguish open
like the eyes of children at the Tisbury Fair,
as if we were created to love beauty
and had just forgotten, or ceased to dare.

4TH.

When America was young and new
granddads still talked of lobster-backs
and sad retreats and fierce attacks
and running mercenaries through.

Young men gave their lives as young men will –
lightly, or for some high ideal,
to see if they had the nerve to kill
and to never know what cowards feel.

And if the slain should arise this day
of fireworks and barbecue,
would they stand before your house and say,
I am so glad I died for you?

A CARPENTER

Wood knows him.
Appreciates the wit
in every finger tip.

With a carving knife
from mute pine
he liberates a spoon
to gossip of soups.

The pupil of his eye
moves back and forth,
a spirit bubble
seeking equilibrium.

In vain.
The world's
not on the level.

When his wife leaves him
his hands are struck dumb,
his knuckles white
with unshrieked grief.

Next time,
love a woman
who doesn't go
against your grain,
and, for luck,
in the meantime,
touch wood.

DAWN THROUGH THREE WINDOWS

The eyes wake last. The night withdraws
like the forgetting of a dream
until the whitening dark
is caught in a web of boughs.
Simple and comic as the young of any kind
the blossoms on the plum trees
fresh from nothingness
spray plump white asterisks
against the pale glass. I rise.

Between the fields of shaggy artichokes fragile with frost
and the exact outline of the mountains now blue,
rooftops bob like flotsam in a zone of fog.
Nose pointed to the sky, the orange crop duster
stands by the highway, parked in flight.
Like the guns of a battleship
that has rolled on its side,
the smoke stacks of the power plant
fire above a cloudbank of acacias.

I would not have abandoned the warm caves
whose changing pictured walls I entered
becoming man and woman, child and beast,
I would not have risen so early
just to see the day be born.
It was necessity that woke me,
work that called me from my bed,
those teeth that nail me to the earth.
Ignorant of such distinctions, from every side
the beauty of the world presses around me
like children around cages at the zoo.

Monterrey, Santa Cruz
February 14, 1972

JAPANESE ARCHERY

by Aleksander Wat

                1.
The hand tells the bowstring:
   Obey me.
The bowstring answers the hand:
   Draw valiantly.
The bowstring tells the arrow:
   O arrow, fly.
The arrow answers the bowstring:
   Speed my flight.
The arrow tells the target:
   Be my light.
The target answers the arrow:
   Love me.

                2.
The target tells arrow, bowstring, hand and eye:
   Ta twam asi.
Which means in a sacred tongue:
   I am Thou.

                3.
(Footnote of a Christian:
O Mother of God,
watch over the target, the bow, the arrow
and the archer).

Translated from the Polish

TO ROBINSON JEFFERS

by Czeslaw Milosz

If you have not read the Slavic poets
so much the better. There's nothing there
for a Scotch-Irish wanderer to seek. They lived in a childhood
prolonged from age to age. For them, the sun
was a farmer's ruddy face, the moon peeped through a cloud
and the Milky Way gladdened them like a birch-lined road.
They longed for the kingdom which is always near,
always right at hand. Then, under apple trees
angels in homespun linen will come parting the boughs
and at the white kolkhoz tablecloth
cordiality and affection will feast
(falling to the ground at times).

And you are from surf-rattled skerries. From the heaths
where burying a warrior they broke his bones
so he could not haunt the living. From the sea night
which your forefathers pulled over themselves, without a word.
Above your head no face, neither the sun's nor the moon's,
only the throbbing of the galaxies, the immutable
violence of new beginnings, of new destruction.

All your life listening to the ocean. Black dinosaurs wade
where a purple zone of phosphorescent weeds rises and falls
on the waves as in a dream. And Agamemnon sails
the boiling deep to the steps of the palace
to have his blood gush onto marble. Till mankind passes
and the pure and stony earth is pounded by the ocean.

Thin-lipped, blue-eyed, without grace or hope,
before God the Terrible, body of the world.
Prayers are not heard. Basalt and granite.
Above them, a bird of prey. The only beauty.

What have I to do with you? From footpaths in the orchards,
from an untaught choir and shimmers of a monstrance,
from flower beds of rue, hills by the rivers, books
in which a zealous Lithuanian announced brotherhood, I come.
Oh, consolations of mortals, creeds futile.

And yet you did not know what I know. The earth teaches
more than does the nakedness of elements.
No one with impunity
gives himself the eyes of a god. So brave, in a void,
you offered sacrifices to daemons: there were Wotan and Thor,
the screech of Erinyes in the air, the terror of dogs
when Hecate with her retinue of the dead draw near.

Better to carve suns and moons on the joints of crosses
as was done in my district. To birches and firs
give feminine names. To implore protection
against mute and treacherous might, rather
than proclaim, as you did, an inhuman thing.

Translated from the Polish with the author
Berkeley, 1963

READING REXROTH'S TRANSLATION OF TU FU

> *At least we shall have descendants.*
>   *— Tu Fu*

A Chinese poet stands in my room
lamenting his small and useless fame
as he has the last twelve hundred years.
The window flares with October sun, dims
with fast October cloud, my wife out
buying in the world, my son asleep.

Left alone, I become noble, disreputable.
My companion smells of wine, thrift, and ink
as he complains how the servants of the great
regard him unhappily from hair to shoes
through half unopened doors. We are rich,
like ugly women, in all the wrong places.

Wishing to speak to all humankind,
finding forty willing to listen, half
who understand, of those half that value and know,
this grievance so inflames us we achieve
enduring wonders and can thus pester
the living for centuries, cadging admiration.

O us poets, us pinheads where angels dance!

THE GHOST OF DELMORE SCHWARTZ

I have seen that moon face
rise behind my shoulder
in the mirror like a bum
floating up from the sidewalk
bribing his own disappearance
with the reminder that suffering
stinks to high heaven.
Money's prayers are always answered.
The bums go. Delmore stays
behind my shoulder as I shave,
whispering like a dust pan and brush:

"Exaltation is an exacting discipline,
a straight-razor shave
tip-toe on a tight-rope
in somebody else's overshoes,
and poets do not only fall through air
like bags of ice cubes slammed on tables,
we are all metaphor, every hour a fable.
My last hotel was despair itself.
Unlit by the heart life is dim."

WORMS

They too
have no wish
to surrender
their world,
all earth,
which they eat
as men eat time
and so thrash
in every segment
the resistance
of the besieged.

Pitiful.

They know so few tricks,
a brave squirm,
a desperate wriggle,
but a man's thumb
is strong
as an ape.

Invincible.

Day's brightness
deafens them.
Pink as rats' tails,
they flee and burrow,
aerating death rows
in a tin can
half full of dirt.

Only a martyr
could desire
that piercing
silver hook
that cannot
even kill them
as they are cast
through alien air
to alien water
to serve at last
a cunning deception.

Knowing that little
of fishing and worms,
it is no wonder
we fear the light
and trust the old dark.

A DAY WITHOUT POETRY

Not a line, not a glimpse, not an instant.
Like a fish every eye uninhabited.
The fat on the old woman's arm
hangs like a white sloth
from the limb of a tree
as she airs her dentures
in a tenement yawn.

Sightless, we raise our hands in greeting
and touch against the membrane
of foetal solitude. The air is a swamp
of unfinished sleep. I hear
my heart knock like a cleaver
on a butcher's block.

Not a second's glimpse of that world,
not a single line from home.

III.

VICTORY DAY

In this Moscow of Victory and Spring
The hard streets reverberate with pride
At outmurdering.

Dapper with charisma,
The last bemedalled vets
Are hailed with astonished honor
By the merely alive in Gorky Park
Where the rain-brightened tulips stand
Like young women waiting to be loved.

But it is the grey writer sipping red wine
At a restaurant bar who waits —
For a young woman who, his heart and watch
Now tell him, will not appear tonight or ever.

O errors of Eros hilarious
To all but those suffering them,
His own solitude now perfected,
Squat idol of a failed religion.

And then through the public din
Of braggadocio and grievance
He hears a woman's voice singing
So itself in every recorded syllable and tone
That he recognizes it at once: Piaf

And he sees that there is never more than this --
A self at its most individual focus
Held against time's shining annihilation
For as long as it can be unwavering.

And art is the last hard press of the pulp,
A grappa, bitter, inebriating, clear.

THE LINGUIST DECLINING A ROMANCE AT AN INTERNATIONAL CONFERENCE

I am sorry, my dear woman,
but I cannot bear to learn
yet another language.

The word *zindada*
will never bring bare trees
on a field of ghastly snow
to the screen inside my eye.

And how could *kanesh*
be the true name
of the blue water
where we stood in first silence?

Even though to my fingers
you are universal Braille,
except with speech
we cannot be done with speech.

But I will not memorize
another adverbial gizmo
to praise you in passion's superlatives.

I am quitting this business entirely.
I have known too many women.
I have learned too many tongues.

FEAR OF HEIGHTS

The void adores the vertical
for the very gift of being –
right angle of sidewalk and high-rise
hypotenused by suicide.

STAINS

to John Teachout

Grape juice stains, as do beets and blood.
Any subtle wince of memory or fear
is enough to jolt the hand and spill
dark liquid on the shirt or rug.
And then you scrub and scrub with all the elbow grease
and old wives' remedies and chemicals you've got,
but it's never enough to blot out the stain.

It's worst of all when something is new and hardly worn,
the least damage seems to ruin it so completely.
There is no damage like the first. Still,
it makes the second stain easier to bear
and every later one less worthy of notice.
For, after all, how, in a world of dirt, wine, and blood,
could any cloth remain unstained for very long
as mothers, sending their children out to play,
know all too well?

And yet, even now, we long for purity and are saddened
by the first foot or tire print on the snow,
the first stain on the Christmas sweater, the child's first lie,
and so are never exactly sure why to love one another –
because we were once like the morning snow,
or because our stains are proof of life and use
and thus bind us to all the world,
for, as a Russian proverb says:
Even the sun's got spots on it.

TO THE TRANSLATOR

By Vyacheslav Ivanov

Whether your prey's Virgil, lark of the fields,
Or Baudelaire the albatross, or nightingale Verlaine,
Remember, no bird free as these ever yields
To lures and traps without great craft and pain.
Dear catcher of birds, without deceit and ruses,
Without some violence, you don't stand a chance,
Though you be friend to all the nine muses,
Shepherd of idylls, and botanist of evil plants.
For another's verse is Proteus, that slippery god.
Quick hands and courage won't do you any good –
Grab the fish's tail, swift, slippery, wet,
He'll squirm and slip with ease through your skimpy net.
So, to Proteus play Proteus, fight mask with mask!
Invent a little treat for us, that's all we ask.

1904
Translated from the Russian

FIVE SONNETS FROM ALEXANDER PUSHKIN'S *EUGENE ONEGIN*

1/I

"When my uncle, a man of rectitude,
Fell grimly ill, he neither wept nor whined,
To force respect with correct attitude –
Such were the limits of the old coot's mind.
Yes, an example for all to emulate,
But good God could you think of any fate
More tedious than sitting night and day
By a sick bed never straying an inch away!
And what treachery could be more vile
Than to jolly up someone riddled with ills,
Straighten his pillows and bring him his pills
While putting on a sad face or thin smile,
And sigh aloud with one thought in your head:
When the hell will he drop dead!"

1/IV

When it came time for Eugene to first taste
The tumult of a stormy youth, that time
Of high hopes and heartache tender and sublime,
His French tutor was shown the door post haste.
Now at liberty to do as he pleased,
Onegin had his hair styled and teased,
Like a London dandy both groomed and dressed.
High society was at once impressed.
In faultless French he could both speak and write,
Dance the mazurka with facility,
Strike up acquaintance with bows made just right,
Clearly a man of both wit and esprit.
What else is there? Society made up its mind:
A finer fellow would be hard to find.

1/VIII

I simply don't have the time to tell
What else he knew, poorly or near well,
But there was one thing, just between us,
In which Eugene was a true genius,
Knew better than any branch of learning,
And was early on his labor, pain and play,
Consuming each hour of his every day,
The cause of his lassitude and yearning.
I mean, of course, the science of amour
Whose praises the poet Ovid had once sung
When he was brilliant, rebellious, young,
And for which reason, inter alia,
He was banished to the Black Sea's wilder shore
Far from his native, beloved Italia.

1/XII

Early too did Eugene master the art
Of troubling even a seasoned coquette's heart.
And when his rivals sought to sully his good name,
He showed them fast that two could play that game,
He too could slander, cavil and defame
And set traps that'd put a courtier to shame.
Whereas the husbands in their wedded bliss
Chose to maintain a friendship with Eugene:
A former devotee of the near obscene
Would greet him with a cunning hug and kiss.
He'd also be treated well by some cluck, old
And wary, and by a stately cuckold
Quite content with everything in life –
His very self, his dinner and his wife.

2/XVII

When at last prudence and plain common sense
Dictate a preference for peace and quiet,
When passion's flames have ceased their riot
And seem at best a laughable offense
With all their outbursts, demands and needs,
The last gasps of desire late in the game
Which even then are not easy to tame,
We still sometimes like to hear of love's deeds
As told by someone else, our hearts roused
Like that of some old veteran of war
Forgotten and forsaken and ill-housed
Who likes nothing more than to lend an ear
To tales of the march, the camp, and the clash,
Told by a lad with a dashing moustache.

EULOGY FOR DALE LANDERS

Of all of us together leaping
you were the first to fall
to death towards which we all are falling

The ghost of your overdose
was gossiped in Boston and Berkeley,
flitted in the vacuum of pity
that could not be felt,
flared up on a stranger's face
like the last flash of health in the dying,
becoming at last a gravestone, a fact.

And no one said
One of us is gone,
no one paused
beside the raw hole
filled with blue air sunlight trees
which is your absence on the earth

As if there were expediency in generations,
as if you had not also been making
the terrible journey beneath conversation.

THE GAMBLER

Entering the galaxy of the casino
(the universe if designed by the Mafia),
he knows that luck is more than the click
of pachinko statistics random as rain.

Believer in a holy ghost behind the flora
of face cards and in the grace of aces,
singular, integral, ever victorious,
he offers up novenas of C-notes,

seeks signs in the quiverings
of a croupier's ligaments, sniffs
the lovesick aura of the blackjack girl,
and avoids all others like himself.

Luck's hero never fears the whisper
of zero, zero, double zero
that chumps agnostic hearts,
cigars beached in ashtray sand.

A lover alert to any cooling
of tone or touch, he stands from the table
certain that fortune will smile to him again
if he worships her with proper superstition.

As dawn bleaches the lobby hideous,
he clatters down the front steps
and plucks a taxi from the dreary air,
easy as an inside straight.

PERESTROIKA

Down, down into the Rembrandtian gloaming
of the Moscow Metro,
escalators long as mine shafts,
tilted, acute, otherworldly.

No love or crime on the Metro
though thieves and lovers ride.
The readers read, the sleepers sleep.
A hurtling waiting stopped only by stops.

It's opera without the fancy plot,
only mood and tone remaining,
fur and sorrow, smooth as kopecks,
swaying in common destination.

Drunk on the spirits of easy atonement,
a pensioned executioner nods off
and dreams of reeds by a river bend,
young again in a row-boat gray-blue.

A bearded Zek dovens over Solzhenitsyn
which five years ago would have cost him ten.
To this day he cannot explain his own nostalgia
for the Gulag's perfection of beauty and evil.

TO JANIS JOPLIN

My friends do not die of broken health
In labor camps by the Kolyma River.

My friends do not light themselves on fire
To show Russian tanks how bright the spirit burns.

Though I could call such men my friends
They did not run to school with me.

I don't know how their voices sound
When they brag or whisper secrets.

My friends die of heroin needling
Death into life through a vein.

They are found dead on the floor and removed,
Dirty laundry to be hung in the press.

But it does not matter where they fell,
In Wenceslas Square or L.A..

Each of these deaths is a casualty
In our war to love the world.

THE CON ARTIST

Smarter than anybody,
radiant with affection,
he massages your weakness
and hates your guts.

As he reads your mind,
that remaindered romance,
he designs himself
to your ideal of friend,
but like a Japanese master
includes imperfections
to forestall any suspicion
this might be art.

Your cash is safe.
It's your life he wants,
but without any blood on the rug.
All he will take is hours
and hours, filling them
with his own emptiness
until there is a mortal breach,
a gasp at your side.

After he is gone
it takes a week
to catch the stink
in rooms and nostrils.

Elsewhere, he is busy
forgiving himself on the run,
his memories of you
fond and few.

THE SIXTH SENSE

By Nikolai Gumilev

Fine is the wine in love with us
And good the bread our ovens bake
And the woman ours for delight
After tormenting us to the hilt.

But what can we do with a rose-red dusk
That suffuses the cooling skies,
Their silence, their unearthly peace,
And what can we do with deathless verse?

You can't eat or drink or kiss them.
Nothing can restrain the moment's flight.
And wring our hands all we will
We're still condemned to miss the mark.

As a boy who leaves his games awhile
To watch young girls bathing in a stream
And, although ignorant of love,
Is pierced by a wanting strange and keen;

As a slimy reptile ensnared aeons past
In a thicket of vine and brush
Bellowed impotently, half aware
Of the wings yet to grow from his back –

So, age after age – when O Lord, when? –
Under the scalpel of nature and art
Our spirit cries out from our exhausted flesh
As we labor to birth a new organ of mind.

Translated from the Russian

STOPPAGE

The last bee
has crossed the fields
of light and shadow

One spider hangs
from a sill
shrivelling in mid air

On damp cement
an ant has come
to a full halt

The sun darkens
a soiled glove
left palm up on a brick

A pine cone
falls slowly
through the earth

The sky is blank
as the dream
of a deaf girl

TOLSTOY AT FIFTY

for Hugh Mclean

Fingers virginal only to labor
smudge margins with rare chocolate,
but today she finds no consolation
in divans, repose, belles-lettres.

Elsewhere, a youth, brow aglow
with ideas and tea, reads ever faster,
pausing only to swear an oath
to serve the muse and outdo the master.

He knows his readers, knows them well.
Her he's seen at operas by the dozen,
and him on solitary benches,
her shabby, feverish second cousin.

Why has nature rich with lusts
granted him such vivid powers
only to ignite ambition
and upholster empty hours?

He lays aside his pen and
in the desert of the heart
calls out upon that God
who hates wives and slays art.

THE POISONER

The napkin at his lips brings a smile to hers.
His sudden death would deprive her days
of secrets and significance.
His salary the salt of irony, he must pay
for the soup, the soup spoon, and the plate.

She lives, as we all do, from meal to meal.
Careful shopper, with an eye for bargains
and colors, she mixes peppers green and red.
Lucky gardener, the herbs rise to her hand
friendly as fish where man is not yet known.
Skilled in the alchemy of shallots and oil,
she could have made a living as a cook.

Shooed from the kitchen and glad of it,
he sits in the living room with the paper,
the day's lottery of money and disaster.
Money the power, money the measure,
money the power and measure of love.
He has not measured up. Both of them
swindled by his youthful confidence,
now they live only for their theatre
of humiliating sofas and bad teeth.

His penance for ruining her life
is not to taste the acid in the stew.
She has studied poison, a domestic art,
and perfected a recipe for that man.
Among the side effects: renewed vigor,
a sense of one great chance ahead.

YOU WHO WRONGED

by Czeslaw Milosz

You who wronged a simple man,
Bursting into laughter at the crime,
And kept a pack of fools around you
To mix good and evil, to blur the line.

Though everyone bowed down before you,
Saying virtue and wisdom lit your way,
Striking gold medals in your honor,
Glad to have survived another day,

Do not feel safe. The poet remembers.
You can slay one, but another is born.
The words are written down, the deed, the date.

And you'd have done better with a winter dawn,
A rope, and a branch bowed beneath your weight.

Washington, D.C., 1950
Translated from the Polish

ODE ON THE DEATH OF YURI ANDROPOV

Thou too, O Yuri, have been taken by the mystery
That steals into us through kidneys and aortas,
Thou too, O Yuri, who had risen from obscurity
To wave at dairy maids and missiles
From above the tomb and glass coffin of Saint Lenin,
His goatee thrust forward in eternal polemic,

Thou too, O Yuri, exiler of minds, hater of rivers,
From whose forehead stray hairs once were brushed
By a woman's hand, and to whom was given
The power to destroy worlds and who destroyed no worlds
Unless we count individuals, fragile as glass,

Thou too, O Yuri, chess master of the world,
Pinning Sakharov in Gorky, striking at the bishop of Rome,
Taking a planeful of pawns by the Sea of Okhotsk,
Thou too are taken by the mystery that infiltrates lymph nodes.
By the thousands, children will run on green grass
Never once having heard of your name.

A FABLE

The soul is a peasant dressed up for the fair
with grease on his boots and grease in his hair.

The faces of vendors shouting over their goods
remind him of ravens migraining the woods.

They all want his coins, at least one or two,
merchant and mendicant, Gypsy and Jew.

Tempted by iron, sleek cloth and roast meat,
he samples desire, then tastes its defeat.

For he can buy nothing, again he's been fooled,
the gold of the soul is not sold in the world.

So, he goes home to cold soup then off to bed
to dream of God singing and joke with the dead.

IV.

REQUIEM

By

ANNA AKHMATOVA

Translation in Memory of Alexei Navalny

REQUIEM

1935-1940

I took no refuge under foreign skies,
Nor under foreign wing sought I relief.
I was with my people all those days,
Together, in our homeland, to our grief.

INSTEAD OF A PREFACE

In 1937, '38, at the very peak of the Terror, I spent seventeen months standing in lines outside Leningrad's main prison. One day someone called to me by my name and profession. The woman behind me, her lips blue from the cold, and to whom my name of course meant nothing, emerged from the stupor that affected us all and whispered in my ear (we all whispered there):
"Can you describe this?"
"I can."
Then something like a smile flickered across what had once been her face.

Leningrad, April 1, 1957

DEDICATION

Faced with this grief, mountains bow down
And the great river halts in its flow.
But prison locks have strength to spare
And bar us from the prisoners on plank beds
And the mortal anguish they breathe like air.
Now, for some people, fresh breezes blow,
While others take delight in a sunset's glow.
We wouldn't know: we're everywhere the same.
All we hear is iron keys in iron doors
And soldiers' boots in corridors.
We would rise as if for early mass
And walk through a capital gone to savage seed,
Us, more dead than the dead, who gathered
By prison gates, the sun low, the river blurred,
Hope still singing its distant song.
A sentence passed, the sobbing is immediate,
And she is at once set apart from the rest of us

As if the life was snatched right from her heart,
As if she'd been knocked over on her back,
But, no, she keeps going...staggering...alone.
Where are they now my unchosen friends
From those two years in hell?
What visitations come in the Siberian snow,
What haunts them in the circle of the moon?
To them I send this greeting of farewell.

March, 1940

INTRODUCTION

It was a time when only the dead smiled
Gladdened at last by some peace of mind,
A time when the whole city of Leningrad
Was outweighed by the tonnage of its prisons,

When, driven mad by torture,
Regiments of convicts marched to the trains,
The locomotive's whistle playing them
A quick tune of parting and sorrow.

The stars of death stood over us
And, guiltless, the true Russia writhed
Beneath blood-reddened boots
And the tires of the Black Marias.

1

At daybreak they came to take you away.
As if behind a coffin I followed you out the door.
In the dark room the children were weeping
As the icon's candle flickered its last.
That icon's chill was still on your lips
And on your brow the sweat of death.
Like the wives of Peter's executed musketeers
By the Kremlin's brick towers I will howl my grief.

2

Quiet flows the quiet Don,
Into the house now comes a moon,
A yellow moon with its cap askew.
In the dark it spies a shadow.
It is a woman who is ill,
Whose emptiness nothing can fill,
Husband in the grave, son in jail,
Pray for me in my travail.

3

No, that's not me, it's someone else who's suffering.
I could never have withstood it. And what in fact did happen
Should be covered with black cloth
And all the lanterns taken away from here...
                              Night.

4

If you, the merry, mischievous mocker
And the favorite of all your chums
In the same Lyceum Pushkin attended,
Could only have seen what would become of you,
How, three hundredth in line, food parcel in hand,
You would stand outside The Crosses' Prison
Your scalding tears speckling the New Year's ice.
Behind the prison wall a poplar sways back and forth,
Yet all is silent as can be in there
Where life upon innocent life comes to its end…

5

For seventeen months I have cried out
Calling to you to come back home.
I throw myself at the hangman's feet,
All for you my son, my unending fear.
This mess will never be straightened out
And now I can no longer tell apart
Man from beast nor sense the hour
When the hangman will perform his art.
All that's left is dusty flowers
And the sound the censer makes
And traces you can follow but that lead no place.
An enormous star stares straight in my eye
And threatens me by saying death comes soon.

6

Light as can be the weeks fly by
And still I can't fathom how it came to pass
That the White Nights have looked in on you,
My son, sitting in your prison cell,
And how they will look in again
With an eye hawklike and ardent
And speak of the high cross you must bear
And of your death which now draws near.

7

THE SENTENCE

And the stone-hard words of the sentence
Fell on the living heart of a mother.
Doesn't matter. I was ready, you see,
I'll deal with this somehow or other.

I've got a lot to do today:
Kill memory, blunt my pen,
Turn my soul to stone,
Learn how to live again.

That's not it either... Seen from my window
Summer has an air of celebration.
I foresaw all of this long years ago,
This shining day, this house of desolation.

Summer, 1939

8

TO DEATH

You'll come no matter what, so why not now?
I'm waiting for you, my life's too hard.
I've turned off the lights, opened the door
For you, so simple and so strange.
Come to me in whatever guise you wish –
A bombshell exploding poison gas,
Or steal up from behind like a veteran of crime,
Or infect me with the noxious fumes of typhus
Or stage the little fable you've invented,
And now known ad nauseum to us all –
The sound of boots on stairs,
Knuckles knocking at the door.
It doesn't matter. The Yenesei River
Still eddies and the North Star shines.
And with each new horror dims
the blue glow of the eyes I love.

The House on the Fontanka
August 19, 1939

9

Already madness with its wing
Has overshadowed half my soul.
It gives me heady wine to drink
And to dark valleys beckons me.

Listening to my own ravings,
Alien, not mine at all,
I came to see that victory
Must to madness now be ceded.

Of what is mine I can bring nothing,
Madness will not allow it.
(Plague it with entreaties,
It is deaf to supplication).

I cannot bring my son's frightful eyes —
Suffering that has turned to stone —
Nor the advent of the thunderstorm,
Nor the hour of my prison visit,

Nor the dear coolness of his hands,
Nor the wild shadows of the linden trees,
Nor that light and distant sound —
The words of final consolation.

The House on the Fontanka
May 4, 1940

10

CRUCIFIXION

"Do not weep over me, Mother,
When I am in my grave."

I

A choir of angels glorified the great hour
And the heavens melted into fire and flame.
"Father, why hast Thou forsaken me?"
And to his Mother: "Do not weep over me."

II

Mary Magdalene, sobbed and shook.
Petrified, his favorite disciple just stared,
But to look where his Mother stood in silence
No one so much as even dared.

1940-1943

EPILOGUE

I

Now I know how faces can collapse,
How fear peers out through eyelids nearly closed,
How the stylus of suffering inscribes
Its cuneiform on the flesh of cheeks.
How hair, ash blonde or darkest black,
Turns grey or silver overnight,
How smiles wither on submissive lips
And fright quivers in dry little laughs.
Not for myself alone do I pray,
But for all of those who stood with me,
In both fierce cold and brutal heat
By that blind red-brick wall.

II

The memorial hour has come again,
I see, hear, and feel them as they were back then,
The one who stumbled to the prison door,
The one who walked her native land no more
And one, a beauty who was known
Joining the line to say: "Feels just like home."
I would like to say each name aloud,
But the list is gone, questions not allowed.
I wove this cover from their own poor words
Which, standing in line, I overheard.
I always think of them, to me they're still so real
That I won't forget them even in my next ordeal.
And if a gag is forced upon my tortured mouth
Through which a hundred million cry out,

Then, on the eve of my memorial day,
Let those women think of me, and think to pray.
And if Russia should ever decide
To raise a statue to me in a moment of pride,
I consent to such commemoration,
but with one condition on location –
that it must not be near the sea where I was born,
my ties to the sea having long since been torn.
Nor in the Lyceum where stood that sacral tree
Where an inconsolable ghost searches for me,
But here where I stood three hundred hours
Denied entry by the powers that be.
For even in the bliss of death I fear
I might forget the Black Marias' grinding gears
And the old woman howling like a wounded beast
For a loved one she would never see released.
And from my statue's bronze eyes, may the melting snow
Stream like tears in an unending flow,
And may prison doves soar in the sky
And the ships on the Neva sail calmly by.

March 1940

V.

IN THE BOOKSTORE

    for Marcia Markland

Unlike SCI-FI and WOMEN, jammed till closing,
there's never a soul in the poetry aisle,
just carpet and air, and the odor of warehouse,
a soothing nothing amid the engorgement.

Day and night we stare at oblong screens
whose electrons irradiate our minds
until they glow like those same screens,
depthless, vivid, quick to change.

The young and old are so much alike
that only songs can speak their mind.
Why then should I at seventy despair
at returning to this art, this silent aisle

when perfect words will always leap
the synapse of the generations
and lover forever wound lover
with the dagger of an adverb.

THE GREEK RESTAURANT

Here I stopped for dinner
and to consider with retsina
the life where I always remain
like a bachelor host
when the last guest is gone.

The waiters' black moustaches grin
as grey lamb sizzles on the grille
and the 8-track bazookie struts
as in those countries where men dance,
where men dance without shame,
and the air is not a mirror. I
was once that country and that man,
and not to be there dancing, clapping,
better considered suicide than that.

I who lost his singing voice,
I who lost his dancing courage,
I who have considered windows,
I who still know nothing still know that.

METAPHYSICAL

I would guess that reincarnation
is about as common as levitation,
or, should I say, as rare.
But, hold it, the whole world's suspended in air!

THE SELF-PITIER

Shrugging off success like any hero,
he dreams of scars and sympathy,
the cheek gash that smiles bashfully
at mouths cooing tiny zeroes of compassion.

Improving failure with calibrated valor,
his blameless leap and heart-break near-miss
bring stadiums to lamentation, his applause.

But he only sips the elixir of minor sorrow,
fearing the slam of true calamity
and the scorch of grief,
this careful half-a-Christ
who loves the swooning comfort of the Pieta
but dreads the resurrection and the life.

TEMPTATION OF THE RABBI

When Cupid, with his bracelets of fat,
and saliva bubbling on lips polymorphous perverse,
wounds the rabbi at his desk
with arrows sharp as rose thorns,

blood wells from his martyred hand.
He tastes the ocean on his finger tips,
the sap of his tree, the drink
of his carnivorous heart,

and blood's brightness long forgotten
splatters the ancient page
which, in a red haze, ignites.

To serve one God is hard enough,
who can serve two? protests the rabbi.
The air puffs and whistles with Cupid's replies,
gleeful infantile laughter, and the finest arrows,
the arrows of a woman's eyes.

THE GHOST SPEAKS

I am the ghost of this place,
alive and dead, this is home.

If you know the light of basement windows,
then you know the world for me. The fire
in your fireplace is pale as a victim's face,
and I am a secret whispering itself,
pausing on landings, trying to remember.

Your thighs and stews and quarrels
offend my solitude and mission.
When you are here, I retire to the vents
among the dust balls, pennies, and dead bees
where I recite the alphabet, or enter
the grey light-bulb on the third floor
you keep forgetting to replace, curl
myself to its shape, and almost sleep.

Since I did not fully live,
I did not fully die. Only
the child in me bit the apple hard
with hard white teeth and earned
himself a death. I miss him so.

END OF THE MARRIAGE

And when it came time to test the vow
And see if hearts were true,
Death was asked: "Do you part them now?"
To which Death replied: "I do."

HYMN TO NOTHING

We,
made of kneecaps and memories,
sponges of blood
jerked by the electrical will,
we, the living,
can never conceive of it
and are unworthy
of its universal excellence.

Nothing.
It is even more perfect
than the indifference of reptiles
climbing egolessly over each other's faces.
Nothing.
Finer than darkness, finer than sleep,
finer than the memory of a table
becoming a table in a dream.

Nothing.
Its name is a wand
streaking groves of oranges and stars.
We think the name
and tigers arise
wreathed in gardenias,
we say the name aloud
and the tigers roar
a voracious jazz
from their prison of stripes,
the blood in their gums
bright as the silence
of God and the dead.

VISION

Over the gypsy camp of my city
Over the unfinished hills,
The rainbow, a cat leaping
From one of its lives to the next.

PSYCHIC AGAIN

I welcome this illness like a friend
from the pre-historic days before ambition
who, with a feigned look of emergency,
delivers me from cavil and silverware
to this luxury cruise through tropics and icebergs.

Now, at home, sick in bed,
I feel full of heaven and the dead,
their voices calling to me
like books whispering to be read.

Oh how they hate death's clairvoyant twilight
where they wriggle like spermatozoa
remembering streets and streetcars and stores.

The occult is second nature to them now
and boring. It's the smelling salts
of raw air they want. Grandfathers
tug at my sleeve begging back gestures
swiped by the serious boy spying
among legs of nylon, flannel and mahogany.

All they want is my body for a moment
or two, to sing again, to swindle,
to run a hand down sticky oak,
to feel a nose nearly sneeze
with a premonition of snow,
to be reincarnated in a laugh
that will make an aunt's head swivel then
turn abruptly back to her coffee and cake,
alarmed by even the thought of such drivel.

THE WIDOWS OF BOCA RATON

pink stucco of Boca
gold of bracelets and sunsets

again Atlantic waves
deliver vast evening
inducing a touch of goose flesh
in condos and timeshares

pink stucco of Boca
last gold of day

more objective
than the scientists of Massachusetts
the widows take their own measure
in narrow mirrors
choosing between the pearls the good daughter loves
and the diamonds coveted by both sons' wives,
then stride to the door escorted by boyfriends or ghosts

floodlit stucco of Boca
the ocean just a sound now

between the residential towers and the palm trees
the night is like a foreign flag,
a crescent on a field of black
specked with haphazard stars,
a banner given no allegiance
by a single soul crossing the parking lot
though they all bear its visa and stamp

everything depends on dinner, how it starts –
with juicy gossip and racy jokes
or talk of gall bladders and plunging stock
in tones soft as Kleenex damp with tears

but if the cocktail uplifts, the service is unsnide,
the silverware and conversation sparkle
and you win the trifecta of app, entree, dessert –
then these are victorious hours
even if the check seems on the pricey side

that night some sleep, some die,
some can do neither

in the deserted casino of insomnia
one woman sits beside a phone whose silence says
we end up as we always were –
scared, selfish and alone

meanwhile others ride unhurried gurneys
to ambulance and the realest of estates,
to be so seldom remembered by sons and daughters
(except the one who loved the pearls)
that it is just as well, no after-life exists
for all parents would do is twist in bitter recrimination
forgetting they were themselves no better

pink stucco of Boca
first gold of day

FISHIAN

In the language of the fish
There is no word for falling.
Even those which briefly leap
Into thin perils of air
Like the flying fish that skim
Alongside the headstrong yachts
Or the arcading dolphins
Squeaking monologues of glee
Do not sense descent as fall
But as continuity,
An act and its description,
Letters in a cursive script.

Whereas we, weak-kneed, are born
To falter and, falling, fail,
As infants learn step by step;
So we make the world a place
Of misstep and consequence:
Rebel angels fell to Hell,
Man in Eden fell from grace,
Soldiers, empires, women,
Stocks, all fall, even the year
Stumbles into red autumn.

Yet there can be no falling
Except from a place above
To which we then seek return,
Heaven of every striving,
Believed by all achievement.

All is wave and only wave
And of course the love of wave --
Isn't that what the fish say
With insistent kissy mouths
Against aquarium glass
Or, when beached and moribund,
They gasp up at the blue sky
That Genghis Khan called God.

DRACULA'S APOLOGY

In my tuxedo of silky darkness,
my shirt front of pleated light,
striding across leaves which rustle
like a smoker's lungs, I pause
by the black oaks, and I wait.

Hoof clop on gravel now,
creak of carriage leather, lazy whip.
Bare as the moon her shoulders
emerge from the shadowy woods.

O my prey, my answered prayer,
you give me the gift of levitation,
the gift of tyrannical desire.
The blood, the blood is almost incidental.

What can I do when every life
is but a nature spelled out in acts.
I regret my essence, believe me.

My only crime is that I call this love.

LIVES OF THE POETS

Evgeny Vinokurov (1925-1993)

Evgeny Vinokurov's life almost coincides with that of the Soviet Union (1922-1991). And in fact he was born into the Soviet system, his father an officer in the NKVD (predecessor to the KGB) who headed up one of Moscow's main districts.

When Nazi Germany attacked Soviet Russia in 1941, Vinokurov quit high school, completed a two-year artillery course in nine months, then took command of an artillery platoon in Fall 1943, all before his eighteenth birthday. War was the great experience of his life, teaching him compassion while revealing the depths of evil.

Vinokurov's poetry is clear, simple, sometimes deep. Plain-spoken, familiar-sounding, free of Soviet cant and deceit, it was always widely popular with readers, fifty thousand copies soon becoming a typical first print run. He won all the prizes and never ran afoul of the system.

Vinokurov had a strong sense that there was something immoral about art for art's sake, poetry that did not take the reader into account. "Poetry is music to which the poet listens in himself, but also a duty to which he is subject..."

Vinokurov did his duty. He was, to the end, a good soldier.

Henryk Grynberg

Born in Warsaw in 1936, Grynberg survived the Holocaust with his mother who by definition had the "right look" and who was even for a time employed as a teacher of catechism. He has written some thirty books of poetry and prose, including lightly fictionalized memoir, to illuminate, and bear witness to, the fate of Poland's Jews, especially the particularly cruel immediate post-Holocaust years as well as the transition to communism.

On tour as an actor in America in 1967 with Ida Kaminska's Jewish State Theater Company, he defected to protest the upsurge of anti-Semitism in Poland and to seek a place where he was free to write. Not long thereafter he produced one of his most resonant works in prose, The Victory. Its opening paragraph is Grynberg at his best, depicting a major historical event – the seizure of Poland by the Red Army, i.e. the laying of the foundation for the post-war world – in plain, matter of fact language, with the homeliest of details:

The Russians came down the pitted clay highroad that went through village after village of which only the chimneys remained. They came through villages of jutting chimneys, sounding the road with long poles. They came on horse-drawn wagons, gun carriages, and slow, heavy tanks. Their heads were shaved clean, their dirty forage caps shoved back rakishly. The wooden spoons they'd made themselves stuck out from the soft creased tops of their boots. When they halted, they pulled out those spoons and ate their soup and kasha with them, then wiped them on their pants and stuck them back in their boot tops again. They advanced all day and all night and all the next day again until nightfall.

Naum Korzhavin (1925-2018)

Korzhavin was a champion of exile, spending 45 of his 92 years outside of Russia, mostly in Boston. He had to leave the USSR in 1973 not because he couldn't write there but because, as he put it, he "couldn't breathe there." But he was without regrets: "I am not sorry that I left. It was not a mistake. It was simply a tragedy."

A tragedy because it deprived him of the company of people who felt the Russian language the way he did, who had been through what he had been through, i.e. his generation, his audience.

Korzhavin's fatal flaw was his greatest strength – his natural integrity, he simply could not help being the way he was, of which he was himself aware as can be seen in the poem Eighteen-year-old, included here.

He was first arrested at age 22 when, as a student at the Gorky Institute of World Literature, he passed around poems the authorities deemed of "immature political content." Thus began his experience of prison and internal exile, which left him with a voracious appetite, gobbling "everything in sight" as a guest in other people's homes.

But triumph was his in the end. In 1989 Korzhavin made his first trip home to Russia, his readings so mobbed the mounted police were called out to keep order.

Alexander Pushkin (1799-1837)

Pushkin's problem is perfection. At least it is from the point of view of translating him. Born with prodigious gifts at a time when the Russian language had yet to take definite shape, Pushkin appeared out of a linguistic nowhere. Unlike Shakespeare who had Chaucer more than a century and a half before him or Pushkin's Polish contemporary Adam Mickiewicz who was heir to a glorious encounter with the Renaissance, Pushkin was without ancestor or precedent.

A natural like Mozart, with a Picasso's passion for experimentation, Pushkin can be said to have invented Russian literature, minting its forms and genres. However, it is the musical perfection of his Russian that marks his poetry rather than insight or image which can strike the modern reader as bland and familiar. And not only the modern reader. Flaubert, after reading some translations of Pushkin into French done by no less a writer than Turgenev, remarked: "He is flat, your poet." ("Il est plat, votre poète.") It was the music that didn't translate, and music, like tone, can be everything.

Born in the last year of the 18th century to an ancient noble family, he had a Black African great-grandfather on his mother's side. A young slave sold to Peter the Great, Abram Petrovich Gannibal, as he came to be known, made a favorable impression on the Tsar who stood godfather to him and sent him off to Paris for an education. In time Gannibal rose to become chief of the Naval Engineer Corps and died a wealthy and respected landowner, possessing several hundred "souls", as serfs or slaves were referred to then. Pushkin was proud of his heritage, "Africa, mine by blood."

Like any good Russian aristocrat, Pushkin spoke mostly French until he was ten but fortunately he had a nanny who grounded him in Russia's folklore and language. He was among the first to attend the new Imperial Lyceum and at the age of fifteen began writing poetry that soon had literary Petersburg in thrall. By the time he graduated he was on a collision course with the authorities because of his poem "Ode to Liberty" depicted as the "scourge of tyrants". Between 1820 and 1826 he was exiled from Moscow and Petersburg to the far south of the country — the Caucasus, Crimea and Odessa. It was a painful but productive time, giving rising to, among others, his tour de force novel in sonnets *Eugene Onegin*.

After the failed uprising in 1825 by aristocrats known as the Decembrists who wanted a constitutional monarchy, Pushkin's poem "Ode to Liberty" was found among the papers of some of the participants who were either executed or exiled. Summoned by the new tsar Nicholas, Pushkin admitted he would have joined in the uprising had he known of it. From that moment on Nicholas became Pushkin's personal censor and never allowed him to leave the country.

1831 was a fateful year for Pushkin. When the Poles rose up against Tsarist Russian rule, Pushkin came out for empire in his poem "To The Slanderers Of Russia" which depicted the conflict as a domestic squabble among Slavs. That same year he married sixteen-year-old society beauty Natalya Goncharova who bore him four children but ultimately took part in his disgrace by flirting openly with a Dutch courtier, such that Pushkin felt he had no choice but to challenge him to a duel which cost the poet his life in early 1837.

Though much of his poetry remains sealed in Russian, some operas inspired by his play Boris Godunov or The Queen of Spades have won him fame outside his native land. A sense of the esteem in which he is held by Russians can be glimpsed by an independent poll taken in 2023 of the most notable figures of world history. There were few foreigners: only Einstein and the two invaders, Napoleon and Hitler came in with under 10% while Pushkin with 23% beat out Peter the Great only trailing Lenin with 30% and Stalin on top with 39. Not bad for a poet.

Aleksander Wat (1900-1967)

My Century, Wat's magisterial memoirs, is aptly named, not only because his life paralleled the 20th century chronologically, but also deeply partook of its dramas of ideology and suffering. He was born into a mostly secular Warsaw Jewish intellectual family, though his ancestors included the Kabbalist Isaac Luria and Catholic priests in Vienna.

Wat himself was a man who needed to believe. WWI had not only destroyed several great empires but Europe's universe of meaning, values, symbols, its codes of thought and behavior. As a young poet he sought refuge in Futurism but more so in Dadaism, which satisfied his sense of the absurd. In the end it came down to the choice between communism and fascism. Though never a Marxist or a party member, Wat was the editor of The Literary Monthly the most important communist magazine in Poland between the wars.

When war broke out in 1939, Wat as a "commie Jew" of course fled east toward the USSR. In the ensuing chaos Wat was separated from his wife and eight-year-old son who were quickly deported to Kazakhstan. Wat himself meanwhile began his odyssey of Soviet prisons which took him to, among others, Lubyanka, the headquarters of Stalin's Secret Police in central Moscow where in an odd respite he reread Proust's Swann's Way and did not find it gossipy and gossamer but life-giving, and was "more charmed than ever by the power of its energy, its beauty of movement."

Wat is to Soviet prisons what Solzhenitsyn is to the Gulag, both chronicler and connoisseur. Wat is particularly adept at revealing the sociology of the cell, how hierarchies of authority are formed, shift, reassemble; how men stand up to confinement and prison's flattened, featureless universe of time. It was in one such prison, in Saratov, that Wat had a mystical experience and converted to Christianity, not so much in place of his Judaism, but in addition to it.

Wat was reunited with his wife and son in 1942 in Kazakhstan where they remained in poverty and oppression until the end of the war when they were repatriated to Poland.

The spirit of poetry, dormant in Wat during his engagee years, returned to him in Poland, winning him both devotees and enemies. After 1959 the Wats lived in Paris. In 1967, the physical pain of his various ailments became too great, and he put an end to his own life.

Had Wat ever found any of the peace of belief by then? Perhaps something of an answer can be found in his poem "Japanese Archery", included here in which three religious worldviews – Zen, Hinduism, Catholicism – enclose each other, an exquisitely wrought poem ending in a metaphysical joke.

Czeslaw Milosz (1911-2004)

Milosz felt history on his skin the way others might feel the weather. Born in 1911 in Lithuania, then part of the Russian empire, he was, at age six in Siberia with his family – his father a civil engineer working there – when the First World War broke out and they had to make their way home across that vast and turbulent land. So, from the very start he knew what it meant to be the plaything of great forces.

Educated in Vilnius, he published his first book of poems at twenty-one and was affiliated with the Catastrophists, poets who took the doom-laden atmosphere of the '30's as an omen of worse to come, their forebodings proving mild in the event. Milosz spent World War II in Nazi-occupied Poland working with the resistance, witness to both the atrocities of war and the moral ruin it can engender:

Having the choice of our death and that of a friend,
We chose his, coldly thinking: let it be done quickly...

In the ruins of post-war Poland – Warsaw had been systematically dynamited by the retreating German army – the intellectuals believed that only communist rule could rebuild the country, at least physically. Some convinced themselves that they were like ancient Greeks smuggling higher culture into Rome. Milosz became Poland's cultural attache in Paris until in 1951 he dramatically broke with the government and defected to the West. He was making history now. Never without humor, he compared accepting communism to convincing yourself that swallowing live frogs was beneficial to your health — sooner or later, the "stomach will revolt." The tortuous justifications of the intelligentsia was the subject of his book The Captive Mind, a fundamental text of the Cold War which made his name in the West. Still, for a Polish writer to support a family by his pen in post-war France was no easy task. He was rescued by the offer of a teaching position at the University of California, and thus it was that the ever-timely Czeslaw Milosz arrived in Berkeley just as the 60's were beginning. He was fascinated by America in general and California in particular, both so unlike anything he'd known before.

The combination of professor and poet proved congenial to him. There was time to write poetry and to translate it; he learned Hebrew to read the Old Testament in the original. His translations of the Psalms of King David are now part of the Polish Bible.

Poland shone, a bright star of history in the early 80's: in 1978 the arch-bishop of Krakow was appointed pope, John Paul II, in 1980 a charismatic electrician by the name of Lech Walesa led a workers' revolt against the communist state, the workers themselves also inspired by Milosz's poem "You Who Wronged a Simple Man." That same year Czeslaw Milosz was awarded the Nobel Prize. He returned to Poland in his later years.

He held himself and poetry to the highest standard:
What is poetry that does not save nations or people?
A connivance with official lies,
A song for drunkards
Whose throats will be slit in a moment,
Readings for sophomore girls.

Intellectually strict, happily voluptuous, his poetry will be read for centuries.

Vyacheslav Ivanov (1866-1949)

Classicist and philosopher, poet and translator, Vyacheslav Ivanov was successful in most all of his endeavors – translations of Sappho, Aeschylus, Petrarch and his own "Roman sonnets", but he may be best known for the book he wrote with another scholar, Mikhail Gershenzon, using the novel method of writing each other "Letters From Across the Room" in a medical facility where there were both recuperating from the hardships of the Civil War.

The early years of the 20th century, known in Russia as the Silver Age, were the apex of Ivanov's influence. He was the hierophant of Symbolism which he characterized, in Latin, as "a realibus ad realiora", "from reality toward a higher reality." Symbolism was thus a worldview and an aesthetic. Its adherents, devotees and assorted seekers met on Wednesdays at Ivanov's St. Petersburg apartment known as The Tower, dinner often not served until two in the morning.

Soviet Russia was, needless to say, not for the likes of him. And since the feeling was mutual, it proved relatively easy for Ivanov to arrange a self-exile in 1924 to Rome, where he spent the remaining twenty-five years of his life — even converting to Roman Catholicism.

Nikolai Gumilev (1886-1921)

Gumilev's was a life of courage. He displayed the same bravery whether hunting lions in Africa or confronting Bolsheviks in Russia, the latter proving more dangerous.

He was connected for a time in 1910 with the Symbolist circle of Vyacheslav Ivanov, attending the late-night sessions in the Tower, Ivanov's St. Petersburg apartment. He quickly saw that Symbolism – a mixture of Verlaine's "de la musique avant toute chose" ("the music above all else") and Baudelaire's view of life and nature as a "forét de symboles" ("forest of symbols") – was not his cup of tea. He wanted a poetry that was less arty and closer to craft, like that of stone masons who build cathedrals, real things visible in the real light of the day. Still, his poetry always retained a certain passionate fantasticality.

In 1910 he married Anna Akhmatova who would become one of Russia's greatest 20th century poets. Their child Lev, who would spend almost 20 years in Stalin's gulag and was the subject of her masterpiece Requiem, became a prophet of Russia's Eurasian exceptionalism, a doctrine much in fashion in today's occidentophobic Russia.

When World War One broke out, Gumilev volunteered and fought at the front in the cavalry and was twice decorated with Russia's highest medal for exceptional courage, the Cross of St. George. After the 1917 revolution he made no secret of his contempt for a communism that favored the masses over the individual. In 1921 he was arrested for being a part of a non-existent anti-communist conspiracy. Maxim Gorky raced to Moscow to ask Lenin that Gumilev's life be spared, but he had already been executed without even the quick formality of a trial.

Anna Akhmatova (1889-1966)

War and revolution tore her life in half, transforming her from a self-consumed artist to a witness of history.

By her late teens and early twenties she was writing poetry and living la vie Bohème, combining the two in the notorious Petersburg café, *The Stray Dog*. After being assiduously wooed, at 21 she married the dashing poet Nikolai Gumilev (see above). While in Paris on their honeymoon in that era of open borders, she struck up an acquaintance with Amedeo Modigliani, then unknown and dirt poor. Later on they began an affair that combined the aesthetic and erotic. They would sit in the summer rain in the Luxembourg Gardens under his "enormous, decrepit black umbrella... Together we recited Verlaine whom both of us remembered by heart, happy at remembering the same passages." Modigliani did sixteen drawings of her in the nude, one of which managed to elude the various disasters of the 20th century and was with Akhmatova to the end.

In 1912, at 23, she published her first collection of poetry, *Evening*, and gave birth to a son, Lev, who she gave to her mother-in-law to raise so she could continue the life of sexuality and spirituality which made one critic refer to her as "half nun, half whore" — a designation that would come back to haunt her.

In any case, that life did not have much of a future. The 1917 revolution and the Civil War that followed swept the old world away. Some saw a new and better world being born out of the violence and chaos, but that illusion wouldn't last long. The intelligentsia was deeply shocked by the execution of Akhmatova's husband in 1921 on trumped up charges. By 1925 Akhamatova was denounced in the press as "relic of the past" and forbidden all publication. She would eke out a living by translation (using trots, from Bengali, Korean and Yiddish, among others).

The Terror would reach its apogee in 1937-38 (since no words can describe what went on, many Russians just referred to that era as "'37.") Akhmatova's son was arrested in 1935 and would be imprisoned, with brief respites (to fight with the Red Army in the Battle of Berlin) until 1956. In the year of her son's arrest she began work on *Requiem*. She would write out the lines, whisper them to friends to memorize then burn the paper copy.

Like many other Russians who hoped for some easing up after World War II, Akhmatova was to be sorely disappointed. Her desperation reached the point where she wrote a dozen poems praising Stalin in the hope of improving her son's lot or her own, but her humiliation was double – not only did she write the repugnant poems, they failed to do her any good. Her son was finally released in 1956 as part of Khrushchev's anti-Stalinist campaign.

The last decade of her life was blessedly normal. She was published. She traveled to Paris to see friends and to Oxford for an honorary degree. She died in 1966 having achieved both greatness and grandeur.

RICHARD LOURIE (1940-) after being awarded the Sneath Poetry Prize by Robert Lowell in 1960, Richard Lourie published his first book of poems *My Only Crime* a prompt 64 years later. He had been waylaid by Russia. Born in Cambridge, Massachusetts, three of his grandparents and his father were born in the Russian empire, though no Russian, except for the occasional curse, was spoken at home. But tales of Russian life stimulated him sufficiently to get a Ph.D.in Slavic Languages and Literatures at Berkeley. He would go on to translate more than thirty books from Russian and Polish, including V*isions From San Francisco Bay* by Czeslaw Milosz, *Memoirs* by Andrei Sakharov, *The Life And Extraordinary Adventures Of Private Ivan Chonkin* by Vladimir Voinovich, and *My Century* by Aleksander Wat. He has published eleven books of his own, including the novels *The Autobiography Of Joseph Stalin, Zero Gravity, First Loyalty* and *A Hatred For Tulips*. Among his non-fiction works are *Sakharov: A Biography, Putin: His Downfall And Russia's Coming Crash, Hunting The Devil* (a true-crime account of a Russian serial killer) and *Russia Speaks: An Oral History From The Revolution To The Present*. He is currently at work on a second book of poems which he intends to finish in half the time it took him for his first.